"An easily accessible guide to a growth mindset that enables children of all ages to understand what a growth mindset is, with a good balance of stories and activities which ensure a child can apply it to their own lives in a fun, engaging way."

Sahra Watkin

Year 4. St Josephs Catholic Primary School, West Berkshire.

"My students loved these activities! They had a lot of fun with them, especially the ones that allowed them to be more creative."

Sarah

Third grade teacher in Minnesota

"This growth mindset workbook is incredibly practical and supportive for children and families.

I really like the specific teaching on the brain. I feel this is crucial so the more it is explicitly read and taught the better. I also think the section on 'The Kind of Person I want to be' is absolutely fantastic. You want parents and children to drive the power and importance of pupil characteristics and this really reflects this."

Matthew Clark

Headmaster, The Robert Fitzroy Academy, Surrey, UK.

TWO SPECIAL GIFTS FOR OUR READERS

AS A SPECIAL THANK YOU FOR STARTING YOUR GROWTH MINDSET JOURNEY, WE'D LIKE TO GIVE YOU:

YOUR OWN GROWTH MINDSET PRINTABLES

8 CAREFULLY CRAFTED ACTIVITIES AND POSTERS THAT YOU CAN COLOR, MARK, AND REALLY MAKE YOUR OWN

+

GROWTH MINDSET JOURNAL PAGES

PRINT OFF AS MANY JOURNAL PAGES AS YOU LIKE TO CONTINUE YOUR GROWTH MINDSET PROGRESS WAY BEYOND THIS BOOK

TO GET YOURS VISIT
WWW.DADDILIFE.COM/MYGROWTHMINDSET

Table of Contents

Dear Grown Up,

Thank you so much for investing in your child's growth mindset.

In case you don't know much about us, DaddiLife Books is the publishing division of DaddiLife.com - the leading online platform and community for dads. The core mission of DaddiLife is to enable parents to best support their children's future and we believe that children having a growth mindset is one of the most important things we can give to our children to set them up for success not just in the short term, but also in the long term.

We are excited that this book has found its way to you and into your child's hands. We are confident that by the end of this workbook, your child will know more about the concepts of a growth mindset and have the tools necessary to cultivate a growth mindset themselves.

This book is divided into seven chapters:

1. Me and My Growth Mindset
2. Mistakes Are Just New Challenges
3. The Power of YET
4. Being an Incredible Problem Solver
5. Trying New Ways to Do Things & Keep Trying
6. Dreaming Big
7. 7 day journal

Your child may be able to do many of the activities in this workbook without the help of an adult, although we urge you to be as involved as you feel is necessary based on your child's unique needs. There are some activities though that will require an adult's guidance or participation, and you'll see this mark for those activities.

We sincerely hope that you have fun with your child while they learn and develop a growth mindset throughout this workbook and beyond!

_ _ _ _ _ _ _ _ _ _ _ _ _ _ _

[Sign here]

"Jobs and careers now exist that simply didn't five years ago when students were choosing A levels or degree courses and this pace of change is accelerating, not slowing down. The only way to succeed in the future world of work will be to embrace growth mindset – the willingness to take risks, to learn, to fail, grow and constantly adapt. Forget IQ or EQ, future success in careers will be defined by growth mindset and LQ (learning agility)."

Rebecca Fielding
Founder of Gradconsult and Fellow of the Institute of Student Employers

"Our children will have what is today called a portfolio career. They will be far less wed to companies, job titles and annual salaries. They will need to take responsibility for their development and their progress. They will have to be brave and willing to grow and expand. They will absolutely need a growth mindset!"

Jessica Heagren
Founder of That Works For Me

"Growth mindset is something that I am always trying to incorporate into my classroom, and these activities made it fun and relatable for my students. I highly recommend this workbook."

John
Fourth grade teacher in Ohio

Hi there,

Welcome to your Growth Mindset Adventure!

A growth mindset helps you in lots of ways. It will help you to be your best self, and it helps you to learn and do new and exciting things!

In this book, you're going to learn a lot about your mind, and how to grow it.

We hope that you have a ton of fun as you complete these activities. There are no right or wrong answers in this workbook. We want you to be creative, learn more about yourself, and try new things.

In this workbook, you're going to learn:

- what it means to have a growth mindset,
- how to look at mistakes as just new challenges,
- the power of the word 'yet',
- how to be an incredible problem solver,
- the importance of trying new ways to do things, and
- dreaming big!

Doesn't all that sound fun and exciting?!

Now it's time to start your growth mindset journey. Are you ready?

Sign your name below to show you're ready to have fun, try some new things, and grow your mind.

_ _ _ _ _ _ _ _ _ _ _ _ _ _

[Sign here]

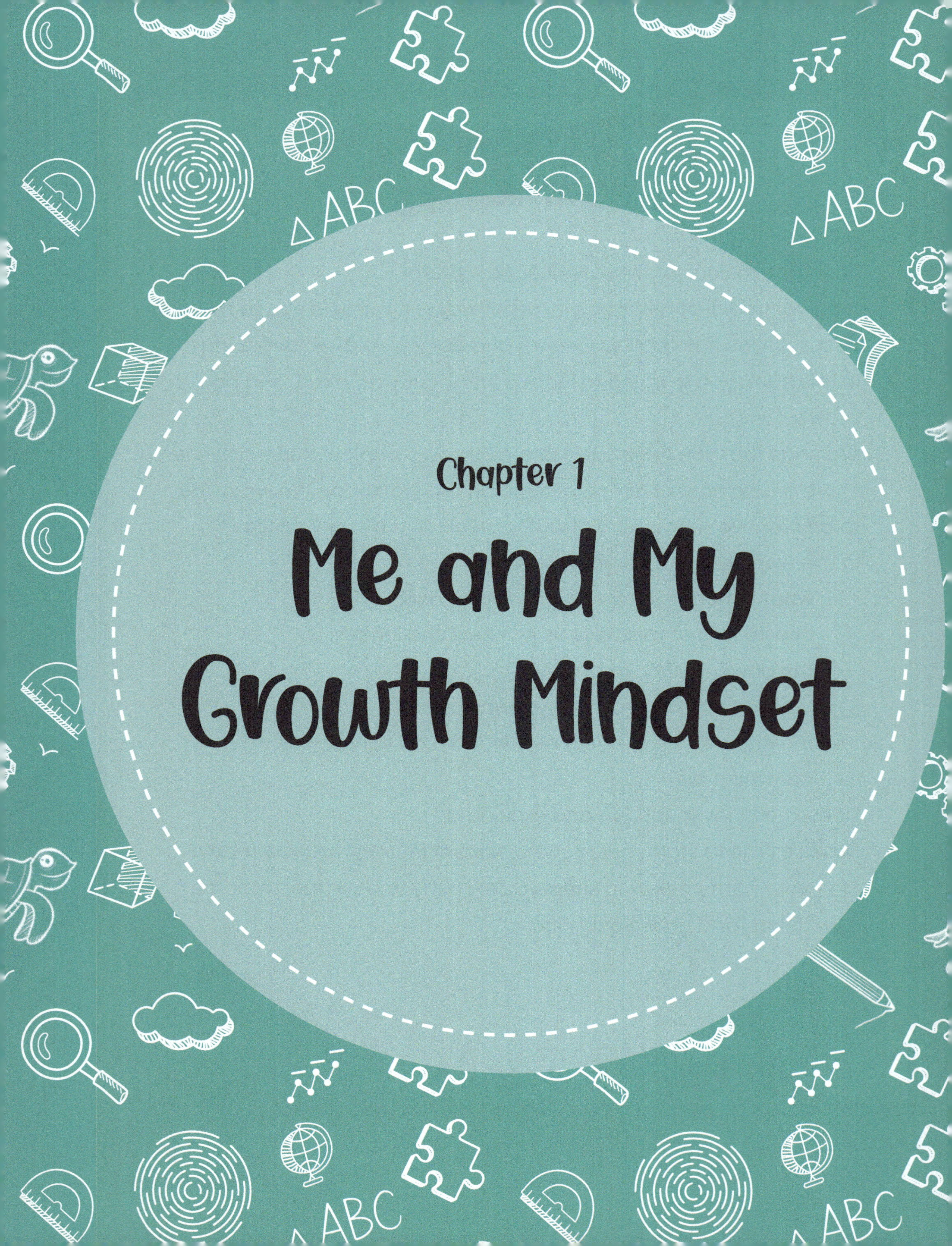

Chapter 1

Me and My Growth Mindset

At the corner of East Street and West Avenue where the sidewalks met, there were two flowers. One was named Daisy and the other was named Rose. Daisy loved the sunlight because it helped her grow. One day, she realized that her friend Rose wasn't as happy to see the sun come out from behind the clouds.

"Don't you like the sun, Rose?" Daisy asked.

"I like it a little bit," Rose said, "but I don't want to soak up too much of it."

"Why not?" Daisy asked.

"Because I don't want to get too tall. Then someone might step on me or ride over me with their bicycle or hit me with a stick," Rose explained.

Daisy thought about this for a minute.

"But if you don't get more sun, you'll stay small."

"That's okay," said Rose. "I'd rather be small than get hurt."

"All those things could happen to me too, you know," said Daisy. "But I like the sun and I want to grow. Growing makes me stronger and healthier. Growing feels good."

Rose was curious when she heard how much her friend liked to grow.

"Is it really that great?" she asked.

"Yes! I love growing!" said Daisy.

Rose thought about it for a minute and then realized that her friend might be right. She decided to try growing a little bit.

Directions: This exercise is going to help you get to know your mind more. That's important when we start to think about where we already have a growth mindset. Put a check mark in each box below based on whether you agree with the statement, you're not sure if you agree with the statement, or you disagree with the statement. There is no right or wrong answer, just how you feel about the statements.

Statements	I agree	Not sure if I agree or disagree.	I disagree
I like learning new things.			
It is okay to make mistakes.			
I am unique.			
I can get better at something with practice.			
I think a person is either good at something or not good.			
When something doesn't work, it's important to try again.			
Some people are just lucky or born talented at certain things.			
Making mistakes is a bad thing.			
When I can't do something, I give up.			
When I can't do something, I ask for help.			

Once you have a checkmark for each statement, count the number of check marks in each column and write your totals below:

	I agree 😃	Not sure if I agree or disagree 😐	I disagree 😟
Total number of check marks in each column			

Give yourself 1 point for each 😟, 2 points for each 😐, and 3 points for each 😃

GROWTH MINDSET MASTER (25 - 30 points)	You already have a strong growth mindset, and understand how important that is to achieving your dreams and goals. When things get challenging, you stay positive, and are open to learning new ways to do things. This book will help stick to that mindset, and even grow new skills.
GROWTH MINDSET CHAMPION (18 - 24 points)	Your growth mindset is already at a good starting point. You have some important growth mindset areas already in your brain, and this book will help those areas become even stronger while also giving you new ones to work on.
GROWTH MINDSET BEGINNER (10 - 17 points)	You're at the beginning of your growth mindset adventure. The great news is that you can have the quicker growth of all the others. A fantastic journey awaits you in this book. Keep reading, practising, and you may well be surprised at how quickly you grow too.

What do you know about your mind that you didn't know before?

Take Away

Congratulations on completing your first activity! Now you know your mind better than you did before doing this exercise. Getting to know your mind will help you with the rest of the activities in this book.

Activity 2

What's My Mindset?

In the story at the beginning of the chapter, Rose was scared to grow. She felt afraid of change and the things that might happen to her if she changed. Her friend Daisy loved to grow because she knew that it made her stronger and healthier.

Directions: Reflect on your own feelings about growth and change by answering these questions.

You are growing all the time! How do you feel about growing?

Our minds are growing all the time, just like our bodies. Think about a time that you learned something new recently. Maybe it was how to solve a math problem, spell a tricky word, or facts about a scientific topic. How did you feel learning something new?

Take Away

Our feelings about growing are important! This book is focused on having a growth mindset, like Daisy had in the story. If you already feel excited to grow like Daisy, that's great! If you have feelings like Rose and are sometimes afraid of growth, that's okay, too. Either way, this book will help you develop a growth mindset so you can be your best self.

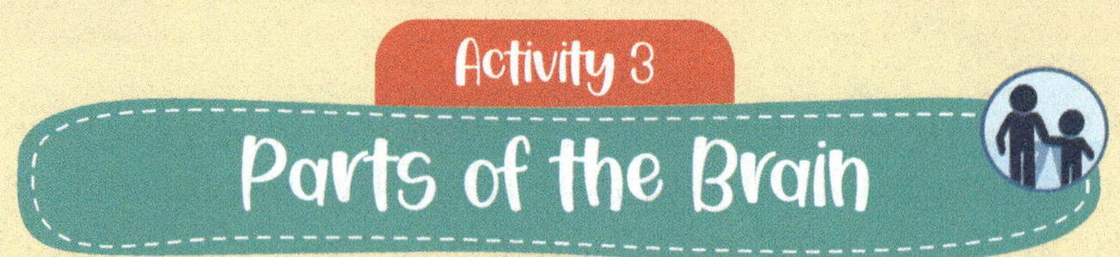

What amazing body part powers our growth mindset? That's right - the brain! Before we start further exploring our growth mindset, we need to learn a little more about what our amazing brains do for us.

Directions: Choose six different colored pens or markers. Then read about the parts of the brain and color each part a different color.

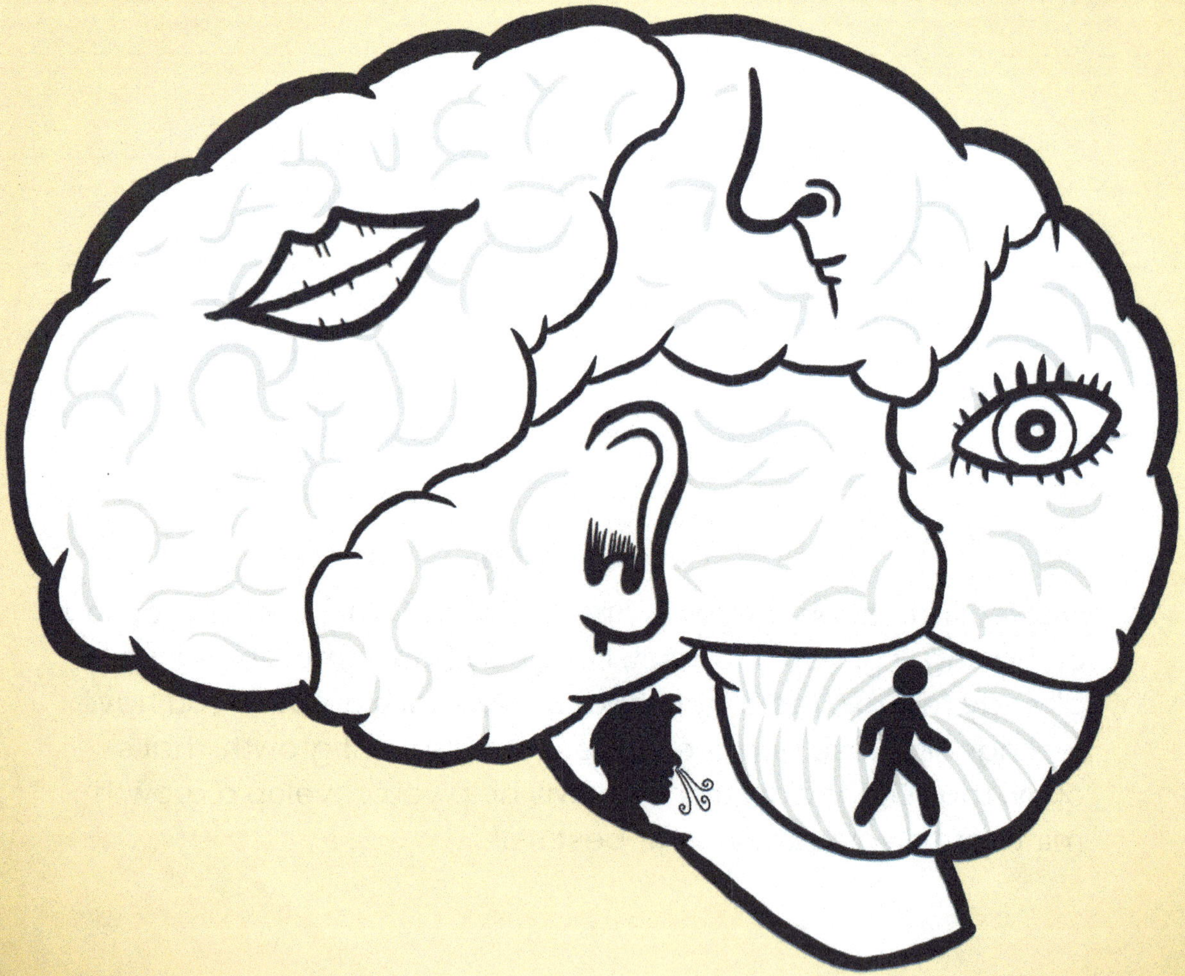

Each part of your brain is very important.

Color the section with the mouth ( ). This is the FRONTAL LOBE. Your words come from this section of the brain.

Color the section with the nose and mouth ( ). This is the PARIETAL LOBE. It helps you smell and taste things.

Color the section with the eye ( ). This is the OCCIPITAL LOBE. It helps you see.

Color the section with the person walking ( ) This is the CEREBELLUM. It helps you stand up straight and move your body so that you don't fall over.

Color the section with the ear ( ). This is the TEMPORAL LOBE. It allows you to hear things.

Color the section with the person breathing ( ). This is the BRAIN STEM. It connects your brain to the rest of your body and controls things that help you stay alive, like breathing.

Take Away

Isn't your brain great?! Now you know all about the different parts of the brain and what each one of them does for you. Your brain is where your growth mindset lives, so it's an important thing to learn about.

Activity 4

My Awesome Brain in action

In the last exercise, you learned about all of the important things that your brain does for you. Now, it's time to reflect on what each part of your brain allows you in your daily life.

For example, with my frontal lobe, *I can talk to my friends and family. With my temporal lobe, I can listen to my favorite song.*

Finish these sentences with an adult and look back at the last activity if you need help remembering what each part of the brain does.

With my frontal lobe, I can _

With my parietal lobe, I can _

With my occipital lobe, I can _

With my cerebellum, I can _

With my temporal lobe, I can _

With my brain stem, I can _

Take Away

Look at all of the things your awesome brain helps you to do every day! Our brains can do amazing things for us, and having a growth mindset allows us to get the most out of their capabilities.

Activity 5

Growth Mindset Cards

Directions: Part of having a growth mindset is being creative. When we are creative, our brains get to explore new possibilities and try new things. Let's start putting that into action by coloring in these cards and return to them when you need a reminder of the words they say. Repeating these words to yourself can help you when you encounter challenges or are trying something new.

There are a couple of extra cards at the end that you can color in and write your own positive sentences, if you'd like.

I believe in myself.

Making mistakes can be fun.

It is good to grow and change.

I can learn new things.

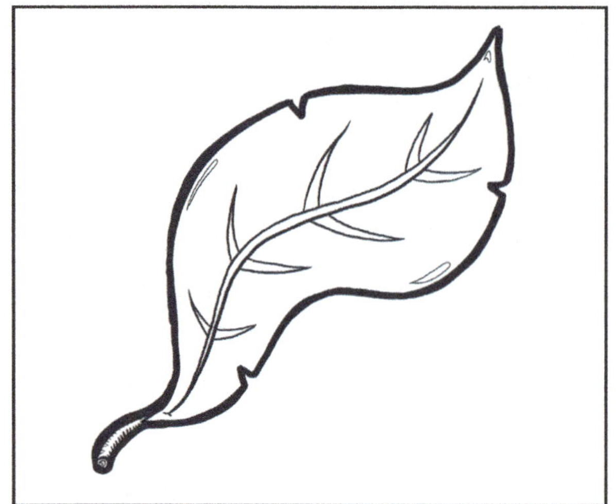

Take Away

Great job being creative! You will be able to practice your creativity in future activities too. Don't forget to return to these cards when you need to be reminded of their words.

Activity 6

Finding Growth

Directions: There is growth all around us. In this activity, you're going to practice finding growth in the world around you. Choose a colored marker or crayon. In the picture below, circle all of the things that GROW. Think about which things in the picture change over time.

Now, choose a different colored marker or crayon. Go back to the pictures and circle all of the things that are FIXED. Think about which things don't change over time.

Once you've circled all of the things in the picture that GROW and all of the things that are FIXED, think about some examples of each that exist in your world outside of the pictures.

What are some things in **your life** you can think of that GROW or change over time?

What are some things in your life you can think of that are FIXED or that stay the same over time?

Take Away

In this activity, you picked out things that GROW and things that are FIXED. Great job! These are both very important things to understand as you do the rest of the activities in this workbook. Keep looking for examples of these things in your daily life.

Activity 7

A Growth Mindset vs. A Fixed Mindset

In the previous activity, we looked at things in our lives that grow and things that are fixed. In the same way, we can approach life with a growth mindset or a fixed mindset. Let's look at the following scenario and compare the different ways to approach it.

A second grade class is going on a field trip to a local park to learn about bees! Most of the students had never seen a real beehive before. Juan is feeling nervous about the visit. He doesn't like bees and is afraid of getting stung by one.

Here are two ways that Juan could approach this new situation:

A: Juan could ask his father to keep him home the day of the field trip, or he could ask his teacher if he can stay on the bus when the class gets to the park.

B:Juan could share his feelings with his dad and teacher and make a plan to help him feel more comfortable. Learning facts about bees could help him understand how helpful they are, and knowing that the class will stick together and learn ways to avoid getting stung could help him to feel safer.

Is choice A showing a growth mindset or a fixed mindset? ....

Is choice B showing a growth mindset or a fixed mindset?..................................

Which do you think is a better choice for Juan and why?

_ _

_ _

_ _

_ _

_ _

Take Away

Every situation can be approached with a growth mindset or a fixed mindset. Having a growth mindset allows us to step outside of our comfort zone and gives us the opportunity to grow. As we saw in choice B for Juan, having a growth mindset doesn't mean we have to do things alone or ignore the way we feel. Asking for help and acknowledging our feelings are important parts of having a growth mindset!.

Answer: A is a fixed mindset, B is a growth mindset

Activity 8

Mind Maze

Directions: Sometimes, we run into things that block our path when we're trying to have a growth mindset. It takes practice to get around these things. In this activity, you'll practice moving your mind through a maze with lots of blocks. Think of a recent time where your path has been blocked, for example; trying to solve a math problem at school, or trying to play a sport without the right equipment.

How did you feel when you ran into things that blocked your path?

How did you feel when you moved around something that blocked your path and found a way out of the maze?

Take Away

Finding ways around things that block our path allows us to achieve our goals. Great work finding your way around the barriers in this maze!

Activity 9

Maze of Life

Can you think of a time in your life when something was blocking your path and you figured out a way to get around it? Use the space below to draw your path and the things you worked around to get to a goal. You may want to ask an adult for help as you think through all of the things you moved around on the path to achieving a goal.

Take Away

Congratulations on getting out of the maze! If it was hard for you, that's okay. Sometimes we learn the most from the things that are the most challenging. Getting out of the maze means you've already used your growth mindset in your own life. Way to go!

Activity 10

Word Clouds

Directions: In this activity, you'll explore some important words and your feelings about them. Around each of the word clouds below, draw or write what the word means to you. Ask an adult or a friend to do this activity with you so you can see different answers.

Take Away

You might have learned a new word or two from this activity. Or, you may have thought about words you already know in different ways. Either way, great job! Examining our thoughts and feelings about these words helps us to understand our current mindset and grow from there. You've completed the first chapter of this workbook and are on your way to growing your mind in lots of new ways! Take some time to celebrate finishing chapter one! Great job! You are awesome!

Chapter 2

Mistakes are just new opportunities

Sam and his friend John came in the back door after walking home from school. John had asked if he could come over to see Sam's new video game. Excited to play his new game with is best friend, Sam said yes.

"I'm hot. Do you have any water?" John asked Sam, as they walked inside the house.

"Sure! I'll get you some," said Sam.

He stood on his tiptoes to get to the top shelf of the cupboard where they kept the glasses. He couldn't quite see inside the cupboard, so he grabbed the first two things he felt. He thought they were both glasses. When he took his hand back out of the cupboard, he knocked something over and a mug came crashing down, shattering when it hit the floor.

Sam looked down and realized it was his Mom's favorite mug.

"Uh oh," he heard John say behind him.

Activity 11

A 'Happy' Mistake

In this story you just read, Sam made a mistake and broke his mom's favorite mug. There are lots of different ways that he could react to this situation. An important part of having a growth mindset is understanding that mistakes don't have to be a bad thing. Mistakes are new opportunities that we can overcome and learn from.

Look at some of these ways that Sam could respond to this situation with a growth mindset and answer the questions with an adult.

a. Ask John for help cleaning up the broken mug.
b. Save up money to buy his mother a new mug.
c. Start using a stool to reach for objects on the top shelf of his cupboard.

How does responding in these ways help Sam to learn from this situation?

How do you think Sam would feel if he responded to breaking the mug in these ways?

_ _

_ _

_ _

_ _

_ _

Take Away

Happy mistakes are mistakes that cause us to learn and grow. When we turn our mistakes into happy mistakes, not only do we learn from them, but it makes us feel better about making mistakes, too!

Activity 12

Mistakes Lead to Inventions

Directions: Did you know that mistakes can lead to great, new things? Many of the things we use today were created because somebody made a mistake. Circle all the things below you think came about because someone made a mistake. Answers are at the bottom of the page.

Post-it notes

Popsicles

Fireworks

Microwaves

Ice cream cones

Chocolate Chip Cookies

Potato Chips

Bubble wrap

Plastic

Super glue

Take Away

From this activity, you hopefully learned that many good and useful things come from mistakes. So, if you make a mistake, don't worry! Something good might come out of it.

Answer: all of them :)

Activity 13

Research about A Mistake

Directions: Choose one of the mistake inventions from the previous activity and do more research on it. You might want a grown up to help you with this.

The story of the chocolate chip cookie

In 1930 Ruth Graves Wakefield and her husband, Kenneth, were running the Toll House Inn on Route 18 near Whitman, Massachusetts. Mrs. Wakefield prepared all the food for the guests at the inn. One night, Ruth decided to whip up a batch of Chocolate Butter Drop cookies, a popular old colonial recipe, to serve to her guests. But as she started to bake, Ruth discovered she was out of baker's chocolate. Ruth then chopped up a block of Nestlé semi-sweet chocolate that had been given to her by Andrew Nestlé of the Nestlé Company. Ruth had expected the chocolate to melt and disperse through the cookie dough as regular baking chocolate would. Instead, the chocolate pieces retained their individual form, softening to a gooey melt, and the world had its first known chocolate chip cookie.

These original chocolate chip cookies proved to be such a scrumptious success that Ruth had no choice but to repeat the recipe. She called her new invention the "Chocolate Crunch Cookie" and published the recipe in several Boston and New England newspapers.

The story of the Ice Cream Cone

In 1904 at the World's Fair in St. Louis, Ernest A. Hamwi was selling a crisp waffle like pastry. He was selling his pastry next to a man selling ice cream. One thing led to the other and he started rolling up his pastry into a cone shape to accommodate the ice cream. The duo was a winner and a wild success. The history of ice cream cones shows what can happen when two people have an amazing idea.

The story of the Microwave

In 1945 self-taught engineer named Percy Spencer was leading a radar project. While testing a new vacuum tube called a magnetron, he discovered that a chocolate bar in his pocket had melted from the heat. He decided to try another experiment by placing some popcorn kernels near the magnetron, and he watched as the kernels popped into fluffy popcorns!

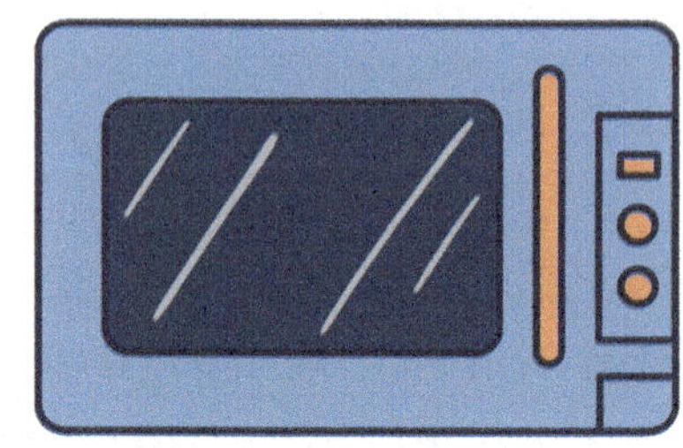

Spencer then placed an egg near the magnetron and the egg began to move from the heat creating pressure inside the egg. The egg exploded and Spencer saw that the yoke had become hot. He realised that the low-density energy from the magnetron could cook food quickly. He created a metal box with an opening through which he fed microwave power. The energy was trapped inside the box, which created a high-density magnetic field. He placed food inside the box, and the heat generated by the energy cooked the food. The first microwave oven was born!

Now it's your turn

Name of Invention: _

Name of Inventor who made a "mistake": _ _ _ _ _ _ _ _ _ _ _ _ _ _ _ _ _

What mistake did the inventor make?

_ _

_ _

What was the inventor trying to do when he/she made the mistake?

How do we use this invention today?

What can you learn about mistakes from this story?

Take Away

You learned more about one of the mistakes that lead to an invention. Great job exploring!

Activity 14

Mistake Interview

Directions: Find one adult and ask them to talk to you about a mistake they made. Write down their answers to the following questions.

What was your mistake?

How did your mistake make you feel?

How did you fix your mistake?

What did you learn from your mistake?

Take Away

Even the adults in your life make mistakes sometimes. It's important to remember that this happens to everyone, and we can all learn from our mistakes.

Activity 15

Write Your Own Mistake Story

Directions: Everyone makes mistakes. I make mistakes. You make mistakes. Sam made mistakes at the start of the chapter. In this activity, you're going to write a story about a mistake you made. You might want to ask an adult to help you with this activity, or you can choose to complete it on your own. There are boxes next to each writing space for you to add drawings to your story, if you'd like.

One time, I made a big mistake. Let me tell you what happened.

When the mistake happened, I felt...

Because of my mistake, I decided to...

I learned...

Next time, I will...

Take Away

Congratulations on writing your story! Now you've thought about a mistake, what you learned from it, and what you might do differently the next time you make a mistake. It's important to take time to think about our mistakes and how we acted during them, so that we can grow our minds to learn from them and act differently the next time we make a mistake.

Activity 16

Feelings About Mistakes

Directions: Many people have feelings when they make a mistake, and Jasmine is able to feel a lot. Read about her story and think about how you'd respond if you were Jasmine.

Feeling ready to start the weekend, Jasmine walks downstairs on Saturday morning. It is cold and rainy outside, so she thinks hot cocoa sounds delicious. A warm drink is her favorite thing on chilly days! She opens the refrigerator and pours some milk into her favorite mug. Then she opens the microwave and heats the milk for two minutes. While it is heating, she walks over to the pantry and gets the tub of cocoa mix. Then she opens the drawer and gets a spoon.

What feelings do you think Jasmine has right now? When you are waiting for something good to happen – like hot cocoa – how do you feel?

_ _

_ _

_ _

DING! The microwave beeps and the milk is heated. Jasmine opens the microwave and puts the mug on the counter. Then she opens the tub of cocoa mix. She takes her spoon and grabs two big scoops of hot cocoa out of the tub and dumps them into the warm milk. She starts to stir. This looks *really clumpy*, she thinks. Then her dad walks into the room.

"What are you doing, Jasmine?" Dad asks.
"Making hot cocoa," Jasmine answers.

Dad leans over Jasmine's shoulder.
"That's a lot of cocoa."
"I know," Jasmine frowned.

Dad looks at the spoon.
"Oh, sweetheart. You used the big spoon. I always use the little spoon when I make your hot cocoa."

What feelings do you think Jasmine has right now? When someone tells you that you made a mistake, how do you feel?

\- -

\- -

\- -

\- -

Jasmine looks at the mug with clumpy cocoa. She wasn't sure what to do next.

Do you have any ideas for Jasmine?

\- -

\- -

"I have an idea," Jasmine says suddenly.

Jasmine gets another mug out of the cupboard and asks her dad to help her pour half of the hot cocoa into the new mug. Then she gets the milk out of the refrigerator again, fills both mugs, and heats them with the new milk in them. She hands her dad one of the two mugs.

"Want to drink hot cocoa with me?" she asks.

"Of course," says Dad.

Take Away

It's normal to feel sad, mad, or even frustrated when you make a mistake. Turning our mistakes into something positive can help us to feel better about them.

Activity 17

The Positive Side of Mistakes

In the last activity, you read about Jasmine and the mistake she made making hot cocoa. As we saw with Jasmine, it is possible to turn mistakes into something positive.

What were some positive things that happened because of Jasmine's mistake?

_ _

_ _

_ _

Can you think of a time that something positive happened because of a mistake you made?

_ _

_ _

_ _

Take Away

Great job thinking through someone else's mistake! Sometimes, when we think about someone else's mistake, we can learn from them and then do better with our own mistakes.

Activity 18

My Thoughts Matter

Our thoughts affect our actions, so the things we say to ourselves are very important. Read the story of John and reflect on the different things John could say to himself after making a mistake.

John is trying to make a birthday gift for his friend Sam in art class. Sam loves giraffes, so John decides to paint a picture of a giraffe for him. He tries to mix colors to make brown for the giraffe's spots, but the paint turns purple instead. John ends up with a painting of a purple-spotted giraffe to give Sam, and he doesn't have enough time to make another one before art class ends.

Here are two different things that John could say to himself in this situation:

A: Sam loves purple and this purple-spotted giraffe is special. Making mistakes can be fun!

B: My giraffe is ruined. I don't like making mistakes!

How do you think John will feel if she says statement A to himself?

_ _

_ _

How do you think John will feel if she says statement B to himself?

_ _

_ _

What is another positive statement that John could say to himself in this situation?

_ _

_ _

Take Away

Words are powerful. The more positive things that we say to ourselves, the better we feel. When we feel good, it's easier to make positive choices and grow from our mistakes and experiences.

Now that you've learned about how making the best of our mistakes is an important part of having a growth mindset, you'll explore what it feels like to turn something messy into something beautiful.

Materials needed: drawing materials (crayons, colored pencils, markers, etc.); blindfold or something else to cover your eyes with.

Directions: Cover your eyes and/or turn off the lights. Draw on the next page for 5-10 minutes. You might want a grown up around to help with the timer.

Time's up! Take a look at what you created in the dark. Maybe it looks like you thought it would, but most likely it's not exactly as you planned. Keeping the lights on this time, take a few minutes to add to and complete your piece.

What were your thoughts when you first looked at what you created in the dark?

Describe what it was like taking something messy and creating a finished piece out of it.

Was your finished piece better than what you originally wanted to create? Why or why not?

What did you learn about mistakes from this activity?

Take Away

This activity helped you learn more about creativity and mistakes. When we are creative with our mistakes, it can lead to new and exciting inventions!

There are four types of mistakes, and we're going to learn about them today. Then, you're going to match the mistake to the type. You might want a grown up around to help too.

The first type of mistake is a **stretch mistake**. We make stretch mistakes when we try to do something that is beyond what we already know how to do. This type of mistake is good because it allows us to learn and grow.

Can you think of an example of a stretch mistake? If not, it's okay. You'll get more examples later, too.

____

____

____

The second type of mistake is an **a-ha moment mistake**. We make a-ha moment mistakes when we realize that what we've done was wrong or didn't work. This type of mistake is good because we can learn from them and do something different the next time.

Can you think of an example of an a-ha moment mistake? If not, it's okay. You'll get some examples later.

____

____

____

The third type of mistake is a **sloppy mistake**. We make sloppy mistakes when we don't pay attention or lose focus. We don't learn much from these mistakes, other than we need to pay better attention to what we're doing!

Can you think of an example of an a-ha moment mistake? If not, it's okay. You'll get some examples later.

The fourth type of mistake is a **high-stakes mistake**. We make high-stakes mistakes when we mess up in high-risk situations. A high-risk situation is something that's very important. High-stakes mistakes aren't good because it can result in really bad things. When there is a high-risk situation, it's better to stick to what we know is the safest thing to do.

Can you think of an example of a high-stakes mistake? If not, it's okay. You'll get some examples later.

Now that you know the four types of mistakes, match each example of a mistake to its type.

Sam wasn't paying attention to the time, so he missed his train. He learned he needed to pay better attention.

Clarissa decided to try to ride her bike two blocks instead of only one block. She learned that she could ride farther if she tried.

Susie added too much cocoa to her mug, so she ended up making two cups instead. She learned to use the smaller spoon.

Tom didn't study for his test, so he received a bad grade. He learned the importance of studying for a big test.

- Stretch Mistake
- A-ha Moment Mistake
- Sloppy Mistake
- High-stakes Mistake

Take Away

Now you know about the different types of mistakes and what you can learn from each one.

Answers: Sam – sloppy mistake. Clarissa – stretch mistake. Susie – a-ha mistake. Tom – high-stakes mistake.

Activity 21

Mistake Celebration

Directions: Because we never know how our mistakes might become inventions or turn into positive creative things, it's important to celebrate when we make a mistake. This is especially true if we can learn something from the mistake that we made. In the box on the next page, draw a party where people are celebrating their mistakes. You can include cake, balloons, streamers, and whatever else you think people might want or need to celebrate their mistakes. Have fun!

Take Away

Congratulations on completing chapter two of this workbook! Just like we celebrate our mistakes, we also need to celebrate our accomplishments! Make sure you take some time to celebrate finishing this chapter before you begin chapter three. Keep it up! You're doing great!

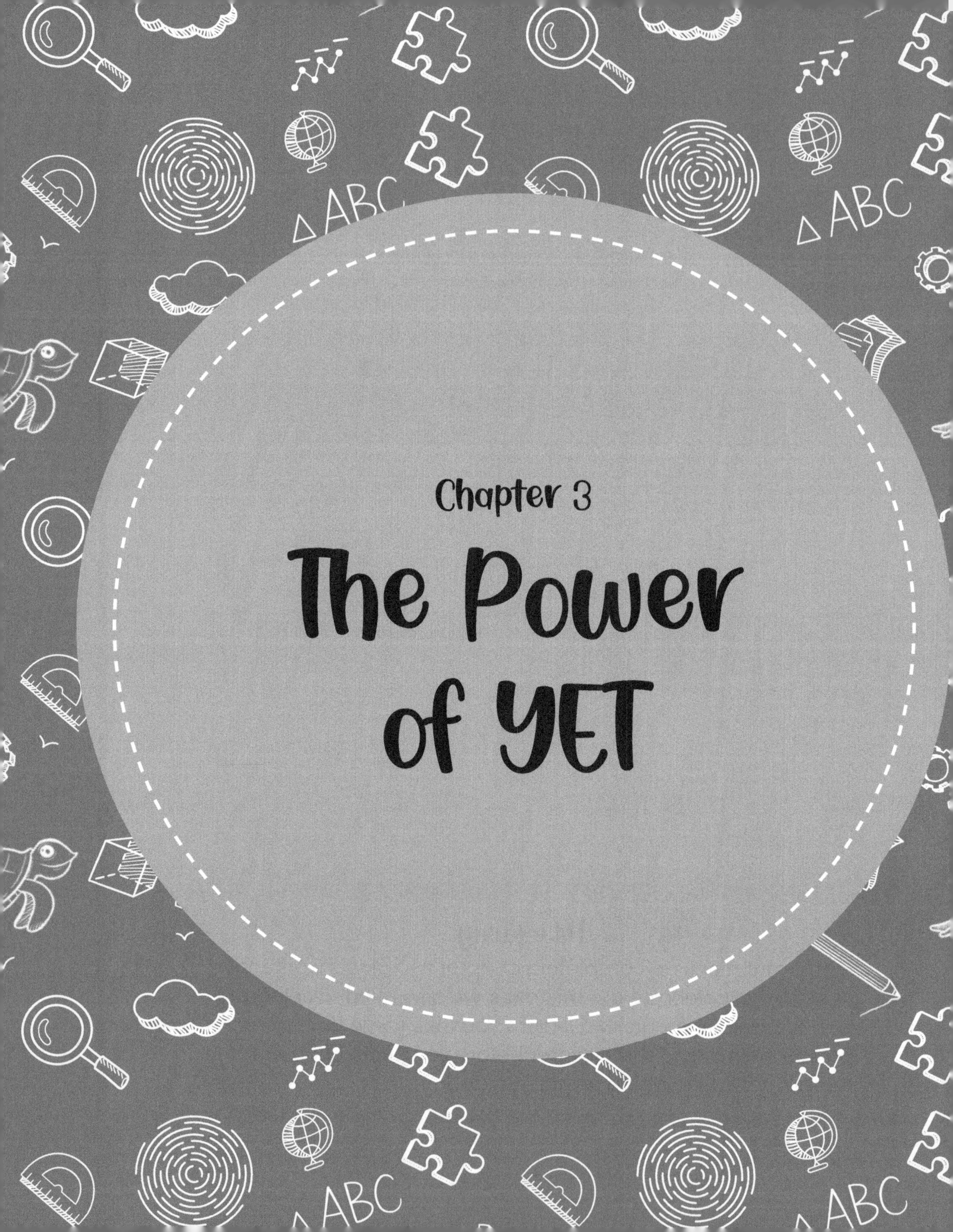

Chapter 3

The Power of YET

Madeline was frustrated. It was picture day at school, and she couldn't get her hair to look quite right.

"Mads, it's time to leave for school!" her Dad yelled from the other room.

"I'm not ready!" she said back.

Soon, her Dad was standing at the door of the bathroom.

"What are yoAu doing?" he asked.

"I can't get my braids to look right," Madeline said sadly.

As her Dad braided her hair, he explained why it was so difficult for her to do this on her own.

"It's really tough when you can't see the back of your head. You'll learn how to do it on your own one day, but I need to help you for now," he said.

Madeline didn't say anything in response. She was annoyed.

Dad's eyes met hers in the mirror.

"You're going to be able to do it one day, Mads," he said. "Just not yet."

"Okay," Madeline shrugged. "Just not yet."

Activity 22

Just Not Yet

Everyone has things that they do well and other things that they don't know how to do yet. A key to having a growth mindset is understanding that just because you can't do something yet, it doesn't mean that you will never be able to do it.

For this activity, you will need two different colored crayons or markers.

Use one colored crayon/marker to circle all of the things that you can do. Use the other crayon/marker to circle all of the things that you cannot do yet.

make pancakes

wash dishes

tie your shoes

mow the lawn

make your bed

sew

make your bed

have a paying job

read a chapter book

draw a self-portrait

play a musical instrument

write a letter to a friend

Did you circle more things in one color or another? _ _ _ _ _ _ _ _ _ _ _

Which of the things that you can't do yet are you most excited to learn how to do?

_ _

Take Away

It is encouraging to see things we can't do yet as opportunities for learning and growth. In this chapter, you'll identify things you can't do yet and explore paths to mastering these!

Activity 23

The power of YET

Think about a grown up you know and write down five things that grown up does that you can't do in the first part of the box below . An example would be, "I can't drive a car."

Now, after every sentence, go back and write the word "YET" in the second part of the box.

YET is a powerful word. It shows us that even though we can't do something now, we'll be able to do it in the future. Going back to our example, "I can't drive a car" + YET means that one day, you will be able to drive a car. It's important to always remember the value of the word YET.

Take Away

You learned more about what the word "yet" means. You've also thought about some things that you can't do YET, but will be able to do in the future.

Directions: Even though there are plenty of things that you cannot do YET, there are a lot of things that you can do now. What you can do now will build toward what you will be able to do in the future.

For each category below, think of something that you do now that will help you do something else in the future. You may want an adult to help you with this activity. We have provided you with an example at the beginning of each category.

There is also a blank category at the end that you can fill however you choose. Try to think of another category with some examples of things you cannot do YET but that you can do now!

Category 1: School

I cannot...	Yet	But I Can...
e.g. Do all of my multiplication tables	Yet	e.g. Do tables one, two, three, and four.
	Yet	
	Yet	

Category 2: Hobbies

I cannot...	Yet	But I Can...
e.g. Ride my bike without training wheels	Yet	Practice riding with training wheels.
	Yet	
	Yet	

Category 3: Sports

I cannot...	Yet	But I Can...
e.g. Hit the baseball without a tee	Yet	Practice hitting the baseball
	Yet	
	Yet	

Category 4: ____________

I cannot...	Yet	But I Can...
	Yet	
	Yet	
	Yet	

Take Away

Good job! Now you can see how doing something now will help you do something else later.

Activity 25

Notice the Mindset

For each of the quotes below, circle whether the sentence shows a "power of yet" mindset or a fixed mindset. Remember, a fixed mindset isn't always a bad thing, but it's good to be aware of when you have a fixed or "power of yet" mindset.

"I'm going to keep trying until I can braid my hair without help."

☐ Power of Yet Mindset ☐ Fixed Mindset

"I'll never be able to ride a bicycle."

☐ Power of Yet Mindset ☐ Fixed Mindset

"This is a difficult math problem. If I keep trying, I can figure it out."

☐ Power of Yet Mindset ☐ Fixed Mindset

"If I set small goals for myself, then I will be able to reach bigger goals in the future."

☐ Power of Yet Mindset ☐ Fixed Mindset

"My friends will always be better at sports than me, no matter how much I practice."

☐ Power of Yet Mindset ☐ Fixed Mindset

"Some things that are really hard now will become easier if I keep doing them."

☐ Power of Yet Mindset ☐ Fixed Mindset

Which mindset do you like more – a power of yet mindset or a fixed mindset?

How do you think you can practice a power of yet mindset?

Take Away

Now that you've practiced finding "the power of yet" mindset in others, you'll be able to think of it more easily for yourself.

Activity 26

Switching the Mindset

In the previous activity, you identified sentences that showed "power of yet" mindsets and fixed mindsets. In this activity, you will practice turning fixed mindset sentences to ones that reflect a power of yet mindset.

"I'll never be able to ride a bicycle."

Rewrite this sentence as power of yet sentence:

"My friends will always be better at sports than me, no matter how much I practice."

Rewrite this sentence as power of yet sentence:

"I can't play the piano well because I'm just a kid."

Rewrite this sentence as power of yet sentence:

Is there an area in your life where you can change your mindset to a power of yet mindset? How do you think this would feel?

Take Away

There is always an opportunity to change your mindset. Identifying situations where we can change our mindset is the first step to changing the way we think, feel, and react to challenges.

Activity 27

Goal Setting

Writing goals can help us to accomplish things we can't do YET.

People who have a growth mindset are SMART. They make SMART goals! SMART goals are

Specific

What exactly do you want to accomplish?

Measurable

How will you know when you meet your goal?

Attainable

Is it possible to meet your goal?

Relevant

Is this goal worth the hard work it will take to achieve it?

Timely

When do you want to meet your goal?

Now it's your turn to practice writing a SMART goal that you can start working toward today. It can be a goal related to school, a hobby, or even friends or family.

Example:

My goal is to learn my multiplication tables.

I will know I met my goal when I can recite my multiplication tables without looking up any answers.

If I practice memorizing my multiplication tables every day, then I will meet my goal.

This goal is worth working hard for because I need to know my multiplication tables in order to do well on my math test.

I will reach my goal by the end of next week.

Let's practice:

My goal is to _ .

I will know when I met my goal when _ _ _ _ _ _ _ _ _ _ _ _ _ _ _ _ _ _ _ .

If I _ , then I can accomplish my goal.

This goal is worth working hard for because _ _ _ _ _ _ _ _ _ _ _ _ _ _ _ _ .

I will reach my goal by _ .

Take Away

Now you know how to make SMART goals. This will help you learn how to do new things so you can continue to grow your mind.

Activity 28

My Support System

Now you have set a SMART goal. Setting goals is the first step in working to accomplish something. Sometimes, we can follow our plan and accomplish our goals fairly easily. At other times, we hit bumps on the road and need help from others. It's important to remember that you're not alone. This activity will help you identify a support system that can help you achieve your goal and celebrate with you every step of the way!

Who in your life could support you if you need help to achieve your goal?

1. ______________________________

2. ______________________________

3. ______________________________

When you have a growth mindset, you see asking for help as a good thing because it allows you to learn new things and achieve your goals.

Why do you think it can be helpful to ask for help in accomplishing your goals?

____

____

As you go throughout your week, consider asking for help if you get stuck!

Take Away

Asking for help is a sign of strength. We can often accomplish more with help than we could on our own! Parents, relatives, siblings, teachers, coaches, and friends can all be good people to turn to when you need help.

Activity 29

The "Power of Yet" Tree

Choose a super goal to put in the middle of your decision tree. This super goal is something that will take time to achieve. Think of something that you want to be able to do in a year, five years, or longer in the future. You may need an adult to help you with this activity.

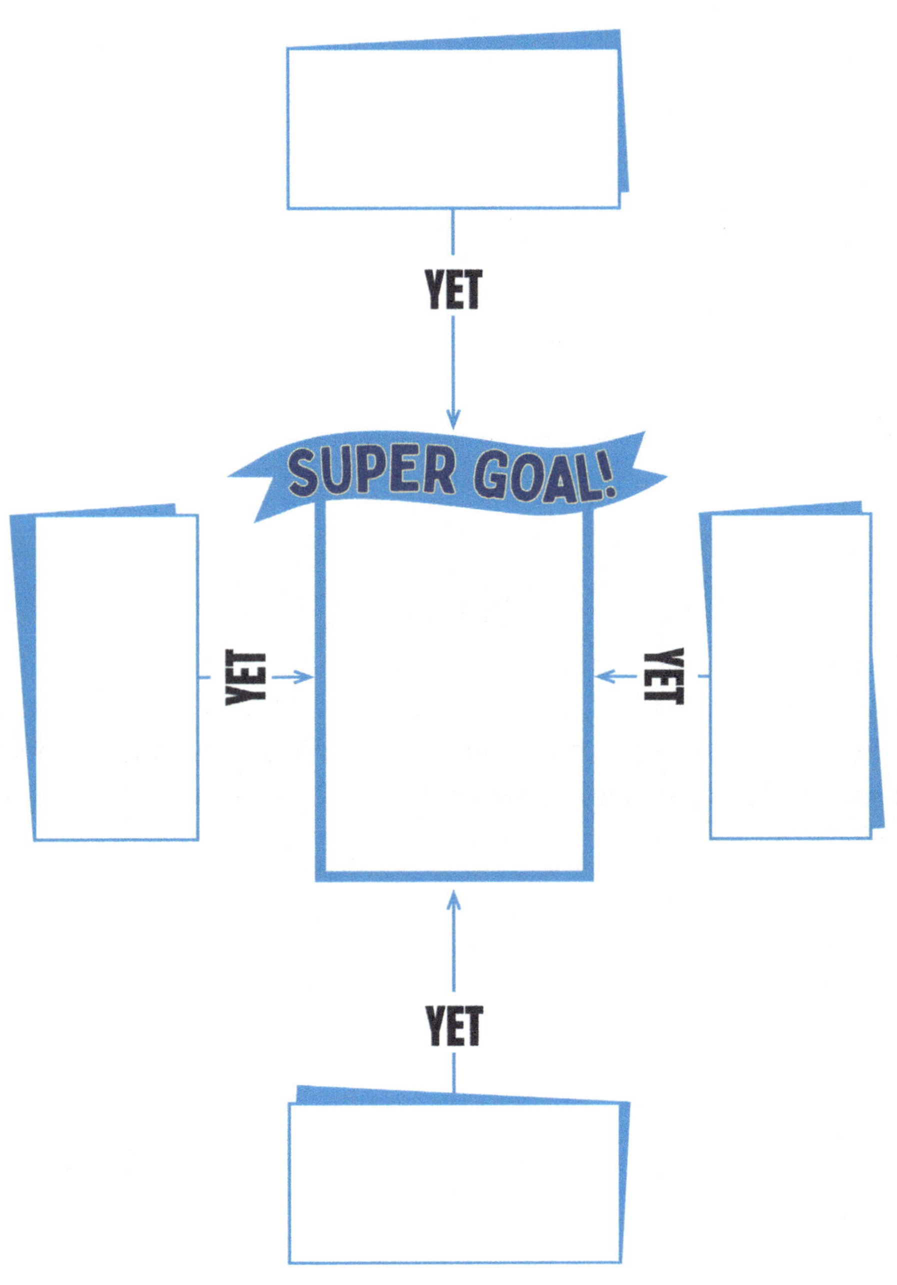

Now that you've determined your super goal, write some smaller goals on the branches that you can do in order to work toward your super goal.

Notice how the power of YET helps you move from smaller goals toward your super goal.

How does it feel to set goals for yourself?

____

____

____

____

____

Take Away

The more you practice setting goals and using the power of YET to reach them, the easier it will become to do this without thinking about it. You're training your mind to use the power of YET, which is awesome! Great job!

Activity 30

Checking-In with my Mind

Wow! You're halfway through this book and have already learned a lot about your mind. Take a moment to check-in with yourself and see how some of your thoughts and feelings may have already changed with the work you've put into this journey so far.

Circle the face that shows how you feel about each statement. (Design note: Show something like these for each statement):

I can practice to get better at things.

I can work hard to reach my goals.

If I make mistakes, I can learn from them.

I enjoy learning new things.

My brain is never done growing.

Which of these areas is the easiest for you to have a growth mindset?

- ☐ Understanding my awesome brain is always growing.
- ☐ Knowing I can learn from my mistakes.
- ☐ Taking small steps to work toward things I can't do yet.

Which area is the most challenging for you to have a growth mindset?

- ☐ Understanding my awesome brain is always growing.
- ☐ Knowing I can learn from my mistakes.
- ☐ Taking small steps to work toward things I can't do yet.

Take Away

Remember, no matter where you are, there's always room to grow! If you agreed with most of these statements, then you're already using your growth mindset in lots of ways. That's awesome! If you still have areas where you don't agree or aren't sure, that's okay, too. The rest of this book will help you to grow and strengthen your growth mindset. Congratulations on completing this chapter! You are now halfway through your growth mindset journey in this workbook. Way to go!

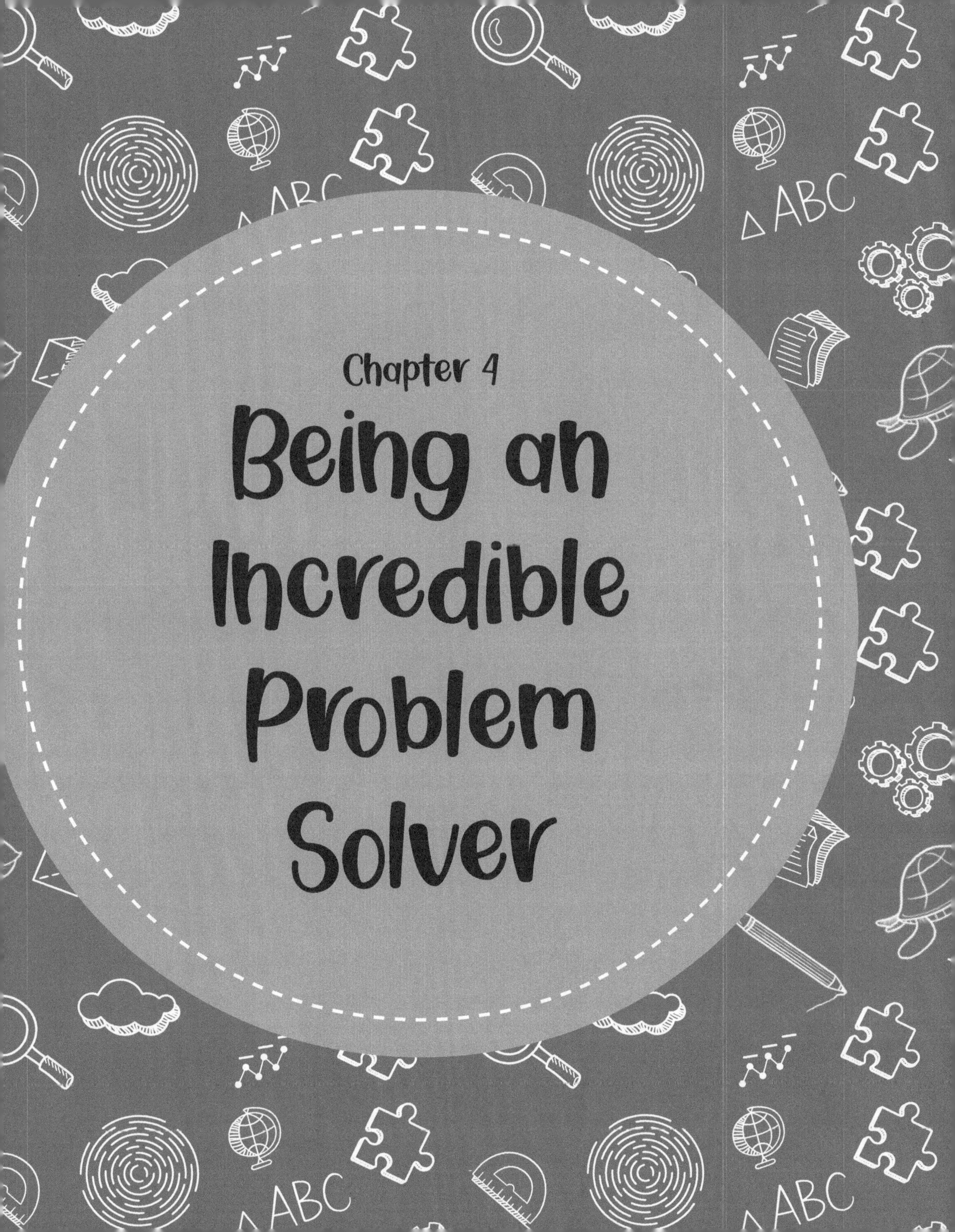

Chapter 4

Being an Incredible Problem Solver

Jade had a problem. Her favorite soccer ball was stuck high up in the biggest tree in the park, and she didn't know what to do about it. She stood there, staring up at it and trying not to cry. After a couple of minutes of staring at the ball, wishing it would move, Julian came over.

"Are you okay, Jade?" he asked.

"No," Pam replied, "that's my favorite soccer ball and it's stuck in the tree."

"Oh," Julian stood next to her and looked up at the soccer ball in the tree. He thought for a minute.

"Can you use a long stick to get it down?" he asked.

"I already tried that," said Jade, "but I'm not tall enough."

"Well, I'm taller than you," Julian noted. "Do you want me to try?"

"Can you?" Jade asked hopefully.

"Sure," Julian said as he looked around for a long stick.

"Here," Jade handed him the one that she had tried to use earlier.

Julian poked the soccer ball, but it didn't move.

"Maybe you should try it from the other side," suggested Jade.

"Good idea," Julian said. He walked back and forth, poking the soccer ball on either side until it started to move a bit.

"Keep going!" Jade was excited to see her soccer ball coming free.

Eventually, the soccer ball fell out of the tree and right into Jade's hands.

"Thanks, Julian!" she said.

"No problem," said Julian. "Glad I could help."

They had a fun afternoon of playing soccer with the rest of the kids in the park.

Activity 31

Word Search 1

As we saw in the story of Jade and Julian, there are different ways to approach a problem. You can either solve problems on your own or with other people. First, we're going to practice solving problems on your own. An example of a problem you can solve on your own is a word search. Try to find the following words in this word search:

Tree	Plant	Dog	Cat	Boy
Girl	Person	Daisy	Tulip	Grass

Word Search

B	O	Y	S	D	N	V	C	E	H
W	C	A	T	X	R	R	D	O	G
F	E	N	Z	V	P	C	B	G	D
E	Z	Y	Y	D	A	I	S	Y	T
Q	X	M	T	A	G	G	H	G	H
P	E	R	S	O	N	M	R	I	P
F	F	G	S	O	V	T	B	R	L
G	R	A	S	S	I	B	Y	L	A
Z	P	F	G	T	R	E	E	T	N
Q	B	H	B	T	U	L	I	P	T

What do you think all the words in the word search have in common?

_ _

_ _

_ _

Take Away

This exercise helped you practice problem solving on your own. Good job! Later, you'll practice problem solving with someone else.

Answer: The commonality among all the words is that they are things that GROW!

Activity 32

Pattern Prediction

Another type of problem solving that can be done on your own is pattern prediction.

For each of the patterns below, try to figure out what is missing and describe the pattern.

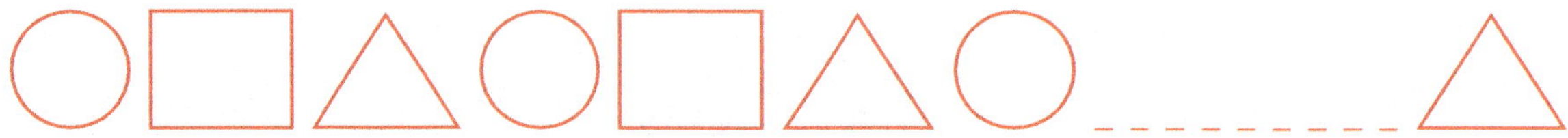

(Answer: rectangle; pattern is circle, rectangle, triangle (repeating))

1 1 2 3 5 8 13 ____ 34 55

Take Away

Just like the word search, this exercise helped you practice problem solving by yourself. Good job! Next, you'll practice problem solving with someone else.

Answers: 21; each number is the sum of the previous two numbers.

Activity 33

Steps to Solving a Problem

Did you know that being an incredible problem-solver is part of having a growth mindset? A growth mindset allows us to see problems as pathways to progress. Solving problems requires creativity, collaboration, and positivity which are all parts of the growth mindset, too!

As we saw in the story of Jade and Julian, sometimes it takes several steps to solve a problem. Being an incredible problem-solver means you keep trying until you succeed. Let's reflect on the steps Jade and Julian took to solve their problem.

List the different things that Jade and Julian tried to get the ball out of the tree:

1. _______________________________________

2. _______________________________________

3. _______________________________________

Now think of a problem that you've solved. List the steps you took to solve the problem. You may not need to use all five steps, or you might need to add a few if it was a particularly challenging problem!

1. _______________________________________

2. _______________________________________

3. _______________________________________

4. _______________________________________

5. _______________________________________

6. _______________________________________

How do you feel when you get stuck trying to solve a problem?

How can thinking about problem-solving in steps help you to solve problems in the future?

Take Away

As you can see from the story of Jade and Julian and your own example, solving problems can take time, multiple attempts, and knowing when to ask for help. Trying to solve a problem one step at a time makes it more manageable!

Activity 34

Making a Problem-solving plan

Having a plan to follow for when you encounter problems can make them feel more manageable. It can also help you to better solve them. Answer these questions to help you plan constructive ways to solve any problem.

What can I do if I feel frustrated when trying to solve a problem?
Ideas: Take a break, take deep breaths, try again later

How do I best solve problems?
Ideas: Working in a quiet space, working with music, learning from others

---

Where can I learn more about solving a particular problem?
Ideas: researching about similar problems, talking to others who have solved similar problems

---

Take Away

Everyone is different! Reflecting on these questions helped you think about how you solve problems best. These answers will help you achieve success in the future. In fact, you get to celebrate those successes in the next activity!

Activity 35

Success of the Day: Your 5 Day Challenge

A positive attitude is very important when you're learning to solve problems. One way to develop a positive attitude is by thinking about a positive thing that happens to you each day. Examples of positive things are:

- Helping someone
- Saying something nice to someone
- Smiling at someone
- Learning something new
- Finishing a project or a chore
- Playing a game with someone
- Making a new friend

Are you ready to complete a 5 day challenge?

For the next five days, write down positive things that happen to you each day. Just try to think of at least one for each day. If you have more, that's awesome! Even if you have a bad day, try to think of at least one positive thing that happens.

Day 1

Day 2

Day 3

Day 4

Day 5

Now, think about how your attitude is different after doing this for five days. How does this activity make you feel? Do you want to keep doing it? Does it help you with other things in life?

Take Away

When you write down positive things that happen to you each day, you develop a more positive attitude. A positive attitude helps you solve problems. Plus, it's just more fun to have a positive attitude!

Activity 36

Positive Affirmation Cards

As you saw in the last activity, a positive attitude can help you solve problems. A positive affirmation is a sentence that you repeat to yourself to help yourself feel good. Color in these cards and return to this page as often as you want to look at them. These words can be particularly helpful after a hard day or when something just isn't going your way. There are some blank cards at the end for you to create your own cards.

I am ____________.

I am ____________.

I am ____________.

I am ____________.

Take Away

You understand how important words are to your growing mind. Now you have reminders of how powerful, strong, and smart you are. These reminders will help you have a positive attitude, even when you encounter problems!

Activity 37

Word Search #2

Certain problems are harder to solve than others. Sometimes we need help from another person. This is where working together can be helpful and fun. Find a partner to help you solve this word search. You're looking for the following words:

Sidewalk	House	Road	Car	Table
Chair	Couch	Desk	Bed	Dresser

```
R O M S U V C H A I R W F N O
K A D D S M E S V W U T Z V K
W T T C Z H U I Q T H Z N H O
G A O R D T A D V R D G H W T
S B T O R J C E D L D D I S W
A L J A E Q E W P A F C E O G
P E K D S C K A D C K A Z S H
Q U R O S K H L C M R R D F K
S H P P E Q Q K O Y K H W E Z
C X S K R R B F Z Y P C E R L
M I O G W T H E P T F O U H L
Z E L P L H M S D U G U T O N
K I B M Q K C N B L N C T U O
U C G F Q I V F J T K H W S X
O G D S Z H T F Y K W L H E E
```

What do you think all the words in this word search have in common?

What was it like working with another person to solve a problem? Did you enjoy it?

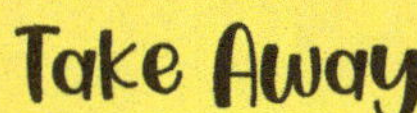

Now you've practiced problem solving with another person. You can either solve problems on your own or with someone else. Both ways are great for problem solving!

Answer: The commonality among all the words is that they are things that DO NOT GROW

Activity 38

Choose the Solution

In this exercise, you're going to read about a problem and then circle which solution you think works best. Then, you'll explain why you chose that solution. It's important to remember that there are no "right" or "wrong" answers. Think about which solution would work best for you and why.

Problem: You're trying to do a challenging math problem, and you're not sure what to do next.

Solutions:

Ask the teacher to help you

Ask a friend to help you

Keep trying until you figure it out

Do something else and come back to it later

Why did you choose the solution you picked?

Problem: You're getting dressed for school in the morning and you can only find one shoe.

Solutions:

Ask an adult in your house where your other shoe is

Wear a different pair of shoes

Retrace your steps from the last time you wore the shoes

Wear two different shoes

Why did you choose the solution you picked?

_ _

_ _

_ _

_ _

_ _

_ _

Take Away

Thinking about different possible solutions and then choosing the one you think works best is a great way to practice problem solving.

Activity 39

What would you do if...

Directions: Problem solving can involve making decisions in different environments. In this activity, you're going to practice this skill. When you're finished, find an adult who you can talk to about your answers.

What would you do at SCHOOL if...

Your friend needed help with a math problem?

Someone dropped their backpack in the hallway?

What would you do at HOME if...

You wanted a cookie but there weren't any left in the jar?

You needed a plate but you couldn't reach any in the cupboard?

What would you do at the PARK if...

You and your friends wanted to play football, but you didn't have a football?

You wanted to get on the swings, but none of them were empty?

Take Away

In this exercise, you thought about what you would do when you had to solve different problems. Great job!

Activity 40

Incredible Problem-Solving in Action

Work with a grown-up to think of a small problem at home that you can solve. Maybe it's a better way of picking up after a pet, an easier plan for deciding family meals, or a solution to keeping your room cleaner! Write down the problem and your first steps to solving it, and then try to solve it over the next week!

The problem I will solve is:

____

The first steps I will take to solving this problem are:

____

____

____

Just like we learned in this chapter, sometimes it takes planning or multiple tries to solve the problem. At the end of the week, discuss the problem, process, and solution with a grown-up. Did you solve the problem? How did you feel about solving the problem? What did you learn in this chapter that helped you?

Take Away

Way to go! In this chapter, you learned how being an incredible problem solver is part of a growth mindset, and you put your problem-solving skills to work! Congratulations on completing this chapter and getting closer to completing this growth mindset journey!

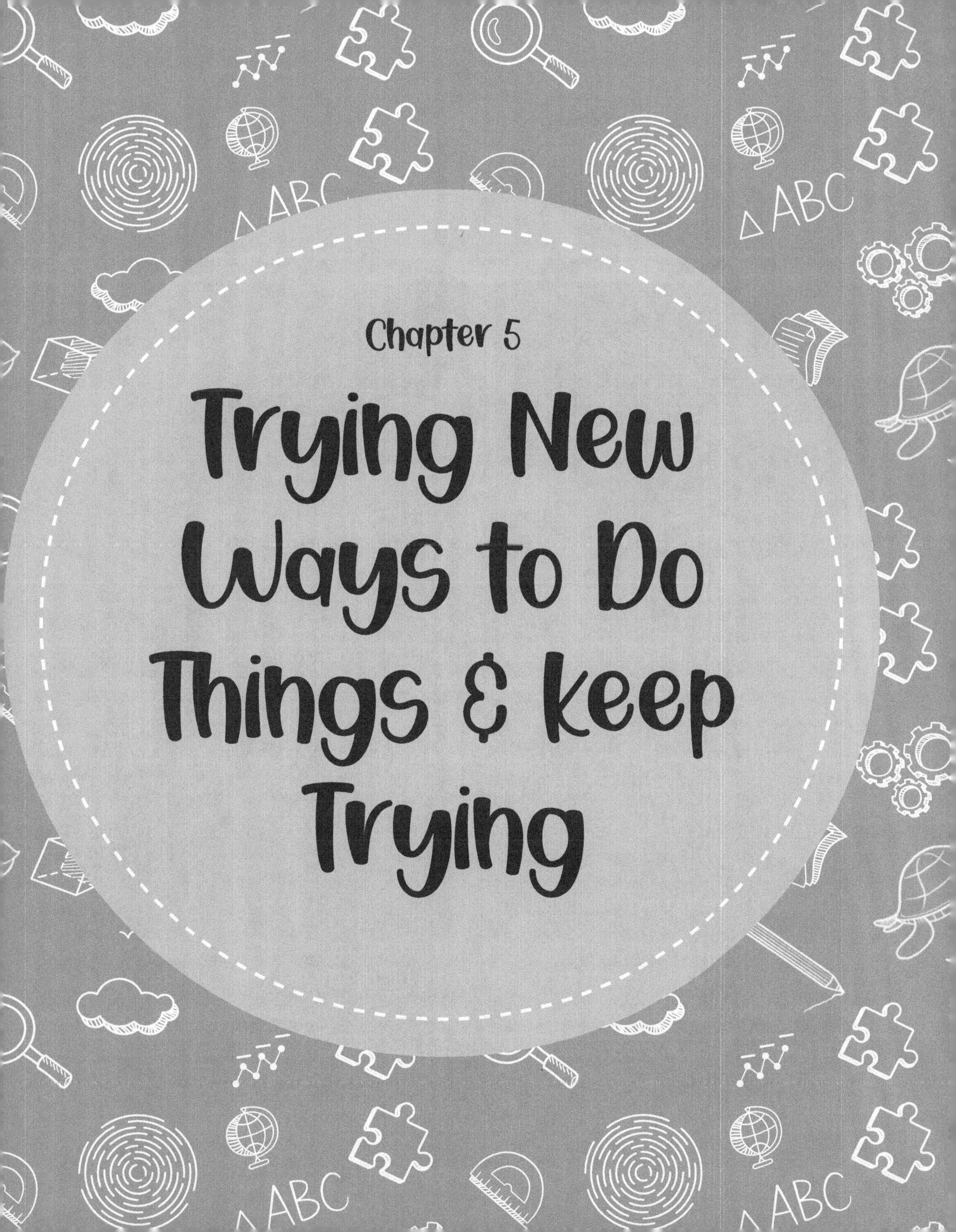

Chapter 5

Trying New Ways to Do Things & Keep Trying

Sarah stood on the sidewalk and stared at her bicycle. She really wanted to bike to her friend Leo's house, but she had never ridden her bike that far before. She just wasn't sure what to do. She went back inside and asked her dad what to do.

"Why don't you try to bike to Leo's and I'll follow behind you in the car? That way, if you get tired, I can drive you the rest of the way," her Dad said.

Sarah thought about it for a little while and decided that was a pretty good idea.

"Okay, I'll give it a try," she said.

Sarah got on her bike and Dad followed in the car. Sarah made it about halfway to Leo's house before a really big hill made her tired. She decided to stop and get in the car.

"Good job," Sarah's Dad said as he drove her the rest of the way to Leo's house.

"Yeah," she said, "I did alright, and I can't wait to try to go farther next time."

Activity 41

Never Give Up

In the story you just read, Sarah really wanted to ride her bike all the way to Leo's house. She gave it her best effort and rode halfway. Right away, she made a goal to go farther the next time.

What did you learn from Sarah's story?

_ _

_ _

_ _

_ _

_ _

How do you think Sarah felt after making it halfway to Leo's house?

_ _

_ _

_ _

How would Sarah have felt after making it halfway if she had a fixed mindset?

_ _

_ _

_ _

Discuss your answers with an adult. Can either of you think of a time when you were in a situation like Sarah? What did you do and what were the outcomes?

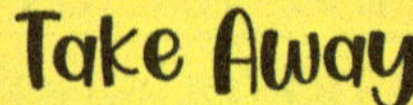

Being growth-minded helps us to stay positive and keep trying when things are challenging.

Activity 42

How do you do it?

Astronaut Getting Ready for Flight

There is a lot of preparation that takes place before an astronaut blasts off towards outer space! Astronauts must complete many hours of classroom training, flight simulations, and physical training to get ready. One of the biggest differences that astronauts prepare for is being in a zero-gravity environment in space. To simulate this, astronauts must train in a special water tank that gives them the sensation of being weightless. Astronauts also carefully prepare the necessary gear and food before their journey.

Professional Basketball Player Getting Ready for the Game

Watching your favorite basketball player on the court only gives you a small snapshot of what their preparation looks like. Of course, getting ready for each game includes daily team practices. Basketball players also review videos of their previous games to and opponents to improve their techniques and strategies. Off the court, they also spend time lifting weights to increase their strength and performing running exercises to improve their speed, endurance, and agility. Stretching is an important part of a professional athlete's routine and so is making time for healthy meals, snacks, and getting plenty of rest!

Now, think of something that you'd like to learn more about. Maybe it's how your art teacher gets ready to make a painting, your dad bakes cupcakes, or your friend rides their bike. Write what you want to learn more about below:

Find a few minutes this week to talk to someone about what you wrote above. Think about how learning from others can help you in your own life.

Take Away

Being open to learning how to do new things is part of having a growth mindset. Great job exploring more about something that interests you this week!

Activity 43

Trying a New Way

Trying new ways to do things is one way to learn and grow. Today, you'll try doing one more activities in a new way.

1. Look at these three ways to make a sandwich. Pick one that is different from how you've ever made a sandwich before and try making it in a new way. Make sure you get an adult's help with this if needed!

   Ingredients Needed: 2 pieces of bread and two of your favourite sandwich ingredients.

Supplies needed: child-safe knife, plate

A) Lay one piece of bread flat on a plate. Spread your favourite ingredients on top of the bread. Next, spread your next favorite on top of the bread. Place the second piece of bread on top of the sandwich. Cut in half and enjoy!
B) Lay two pieces of bread side by side on a plate. Spread your first favourite ingredient on one side and your next favorite on the other. Press each ingredient together. Take a bite and try your tasty sandwich!
C) Take one piece of bread and spread your first favourite ingredient on the bread. Fold the piece of bread in half. Take the other piece of bread and repeat with your next favourite ingredient. Find a spot to eat your snack!

2. Here you will find three different ways to care for a plant over the next week. Choose one that you've never tried before and follow through with it for a full week.

Supplies needed: indoor plant, watering can

A) Fill up a watering can and water the plant once daily until the soil is damp.
B) Look at the weather forecast. Move the plant outside each day that it will rain this week. If it is not going to rain, then water with a watering can.
C) Carry the plant to a sink and give the plant just enough water to keep the soil moist. Repeat each day that the soil feels dry.

3. Did you know that there are lots of things you could include in a letter to someone? Choose a friend or family member to write a letter to today. Then, pick a new way to complete the letter.

A) Write a letter of questions and answers. Ask at least 3 questions in your letter, and tell your answers to them, too!
B) Write a rebus letter! This means use words and pictures in your letter. For example, if you write, I have a soccer game today, draw a soccer ball in place of the word soccer. (design note: should show an example with this image in the actual book)
C) Write a make believe story as a letter. Start like this, "Dear Sam, I wrote a make believe story for you. I hope you like it! Once upon a time, there was a large dragon that lived in a dark forest."

What did you learn by trying something a new way? Talk about your answer with an adult.

Take Away

The same tasks can be completed in different ways. Being open to learning and trying new ways of doing things can be helpful and fun. Hopefully, you enjoyed trying something a new way today!

Activity 44

Bravery Mountain

Directions: In this activity, you are going to choose a new skill that you want to learn or a fear that you want to conquer. That achievement goes at the top of the mountain. Then, you're going to write in different things you need to do to get to the top of the mountain. You might want to have an adult help you with this activity. Make sure you challenge yourself to accomplish something that will require you to be brave!

Take Away

This activity taught you how to set small and large goals. You also figured out how to use small goals to make progress toward your large goals. Great job!

Activity 45

Adventure Log

It takes bravery to try new things! Thinking about times when you have tried something new in the past can give you confidence to keep trying in the future. The next few pages include places for you to record your brave moments. You can write them down or draw them in picture form.

Some examples might include

-starting at a new school

-making a new friend

-trying a sport for the first time

-coming up with a science experiment

-testing out a new recipe

Date: ___________________

Brave Moment: ________________

____

____

____

What I learned from this Brave Moment: ________________

____

____

____

Date: ____________________

Brave Moment: ________________

____

____

____

What I learned from this Brave Moment: ________________

____

____

____

Date: ____________________

Brave Moment: ________________

____

____

____

What I learned from this Brave Moment: ________________

____

____

____

Date: ____________________

Brave Moment: ________________

____

____

____

What I learned from this Brave Moment: ________________

____

____

____

Date: ____________________

Brave Moment: ________________

____

____

____

What I learned from this Brave Moment: ________________

____

____

____

This activity allowed you to think back to times when you have been brave and learn from those moments. Learning from our bravery is another way that we grow our minds.

Activity 46

Keep Trying

In order to try new things and keep trying during challenging moments, it helps to think positively. In this activity, we are going to think of ways to change negative thoughts into positive ones.

Sebastian plants a vegetable garden with his grandmother. After one week, nothing seems to be growing. He thinks to himself, "These vegetables will never grow."

What could Sebastian say to himself in this moment to shift to a positive way of thinking?

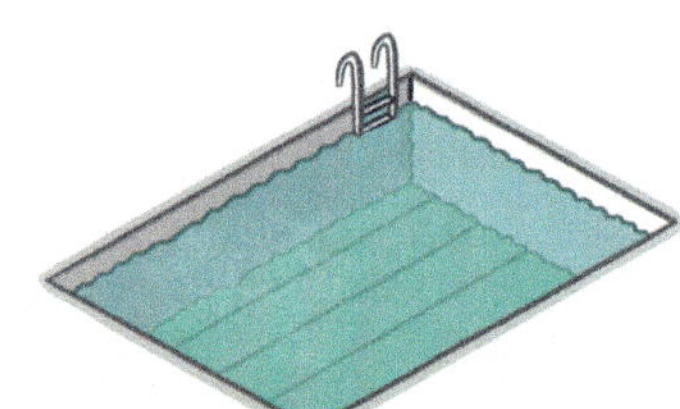

Mya joins the swim team at her school. At the first practice, she realizes that she is the only one who doesn't know how to do the butterfly stroke. She thinks, "Maybe I should've joined the soccer team instead."

What could Mya say to herself in this moment to shift to a positive way of thinking?

Liam and his twin brother are making birdhouses for their backyard. Liam's brother finishes his way before Liam does. Liam thinks, "My brother is so much better at this than I am!"

What could Liam say to himself in this moment to shift to a positive way of thinking?

_ _

_ _

_ _

Take Away

This activity allowed you to think back to times when you have been brave and learn from those moments. Learning from our bravery is another way that we grow our minds.

Activity 47

Self-Talk Exercise

In this activity, we are going to change the negatives into positives. You may need an adult to help you with this activity.

Sometimes, people say bad or negative things about us. Other times, we say bad or negative things about ourselves. It can be difficult to remember these moments, but it's good practice to change the negatives into positives.

In the left column, write down all the bad or negative things people say about you or that you say about yourself. Then, practice turning those statements into good or positive things.

Negative Self-Talk	Positive Self-Talk
Ex: I will never be able to ride a bike without training wheels.	Ex: If I keep practicing, I will be able to do it one day.

Take Away

Changing negatives into positives is challenging, but it helps us develop a positive mindset, which is an important part of a growth mindset. In this exercise, you practiced this challenging skill.

Activity 48

Conquering Your Fears

Courage is the ability to do something that scares you. In this exercise, you are going to practice courage. Find an adult to do this exercise with you.

First, write down some things that scare you:

- -

- -

- -

- -

Next, have the adult who is helping you write down some things that scare them:

- -

- -

- -

- -

Now, talk with your adult about how you both feel when you are scared. Try to write down some of these feelings.

- -

- -

Take Away

Everyone has things that scare them. Our feelings about these things are important. In the next exercises, you'll work through steps to dealing with these fears and feelings in productive ways.

Activity 49

Build a Bridge

In the last activity you explored things that scare you and your feelings about them. Now, you'll use this bridge to brainstorm how you might conquer your fear and the feelings that you have when you're afraid. Draw your fear or your feelings under the bridge and then draw yourself overcoming that fear by going across the bridge. Think about what you could do to get across the bridge and overcome your fear with courage.

Take Away

Thinking about your fears and how to conquer them in advance helps you be ready to conquer them when they happen in the future. This can be a difficult thing to do. You should feel proud of completing this exercise! This also marks the end of Chapter 5, which means you only have one chapter left! Keep going to dream big and further your growth mindset journey!

Chapter 6

Dreaming Big

David wanted to be an astronaut when he grew up.

He read books about astronauts. His bedroom was astronaut-themed with glow-in-the-dark stars, bed sheets with planets, and pictures of famous astronauts on the walls.

David watched movies and shows about astronauts.

His favorite subject in school was science. He knew all about the planets and stars and outer space.

David daydreamed about learning more in school, going to astronaut training, and then one day going into space.

He surrounded himself with information about everything that had anything to do with being an astronaut.

David's big dream was to become an astronaut and he knew he could do it.

Activity 50

David's Big Dream

Use the following questions to help you reflect on the story about David you just read.

What was David's big dream for when he grew up?

What were some things David did or planned to do that support his dream?

What is one more thing David could do to help him work toward his dream?

Having goals and dreams helps us give purpose and direction. In this chapter, you'll get to explore your own dreams for the near and distant future!

Activity 51

I AM Drawing

Find an adult to do this activity with you. In the first box, write your name in big letters at the top. In the second box, write the adult's name in big letters at the top. Then, you write down all the positive things about the adult on the second page. When you're finished, give the workbook to the adult and they write down all the positive things about you on the first page. After, exchange pages and read the positive things you each have to say about the other.

Take Away

In this exercise, you thought about different parts of your life and wrote down your hopes and dreams for each part. Isn't dreaming about the future fun and exciting? Having a growth mindset allows us to dream big and then take steps to achieve our dreams.

Activity 52

Picture Your Future Self

In this exercise, you're going to think beyond the next year. Think about yourself in 5, 10, 15, and 20 years from now. Picture your surroundings. Where do you live? Do you have a pet? If you have a job, what is it? Who do you live with? If you're old enough to drive, what kind of car do you have? In the boxes below, draw some pictures of future versions of yourself.

Take Away

When you dream big about your future, you develop motivation, or the desire to reach your goals. Motivation helps you work toward your dreams and goals, which is an important part of a growth mindset. Isn't it fun to dream about the future?!

Activity 53

The Kind of Person I Want to Be

In the last activity, you pictured your future self and surroundings. In this activity, you'll consider the kind of person you want to be in the future.

How would you want others to describe your future self?

_ _

_ _

_ _

_ _

List 3-5 words that you hope will describe your future self.

1. _

2. _

3. _

4. _

5. _

Take Away

Just like it is important to dream about your future accomplishments, it is valuable to reflect on the kind of person you want to be. Having a clear idea of this helps guide your thoughts and actions.

Activity 54

Dreams for Me

Interview two important adults in your life to ask what their hopes and dreams are for you.

Adult 1: ____

What are your hopes and dreams for me now and in the future?

____

____

____

____

Adult 2: ____

What are your hopes and dreams for me now and in the future?

____

____

____

____

Reflection: Were the hopes and dreams of the adults you interviewed similar or different than your hopes and dreams for yourself?

____

Take Away

Hearing the hopes and dreams that our loved ones have for us can help guide us in finding and realizing our own hopes and dreams. The people in your life believe in you and your dreams!

Activity 55

Role models

Role models help us to dream big. Their accomplishments and stories help us to believe that we can achieve great things, too.

Who is one of your role models?

It could be someone you know personally, like a parent, teacher, coach, or relative. Or, it could be someone that you've never met like a famous leader, professional athlete, or historical figure.

_ _

What qualities does this person possess that you aspire to?

_ _

_ _

_ _

What accomplishments from this person's life are you inspired by?

_ _

_ _

_ _

Take Away

Learning about people that possess the qualities we aspire to can help us to dream big, too.

Activity 56

Color the Quotes

This page includes some famous quotes about dreaming big and reaching your goals. Use this page to color in the quotes, draw pictures around them, and be creative!

"Think big, dream big, believe big, and the results will be big!" -Ikrama Akhtar

"You have to dream big before doing big." – Saif Reymen

"All our dreams can come true, if we have the courage to pursue them." – Walt Disney

"Do something today that your future self will thank you for." -Sean Patrick Flanery

"Dreams come in a size to big so that we may grow into them." -Josie Bisse

"You must dream big and dream often. Take risks and see what happens." -Debasish Mrida

Take Away

The words of other people can be very motivating and inspirational to us. Return to these quotes and your beautiful coloring when you need some encouragement to dream big!

Activity 57

Create A Vision Board

A vision board is a collection of images that represent goals and dreams. You can cut out pictures from magazines or write words or draw pictures that help you stay positive and move toward your goals and dreams. Looking at a vision board often helps you keep a positive mindset.

First, think about a goal or a dream that you want to focus on in your vision board. Write it down here:

_ _

_ _

_ _

Now, gather things that you want to put on your vision board. Ask an adult if there are some magazines or newspapers you can use for pictures or words. You may need to ask for help using scissors to cut things out of these newspapers or magazines.

Try to find things that make you feel happy and positive and relate toward your goals. The next page is devoted to your vision board. Paste, write, draw, and color whatever you want here. Be creative!

Take Away

Creating a vision board allows you to dream big, be creative, and stay positive toward your goals. Return to this vision board when you need encouragement. Create more vision boards if you enjoyed this activity!

Activity 58

Bucket List

Bucket lists are lists of things that we want to see and do within a certain time frame. You can make a bucket list for the month, year, or your whole life. On the next page, you're going to make a bucket list for a time frame that you choose. Think about all the places you want to go, people you want to see, and things you want to do. You can draw pictures or write words in the bucket, whichever you want. Dream big!

Take Away

Making a bucket list allows you to think about the future and your goals in a different way. It's fun to think about how many things you can do, people you can see, and places you can go! Keep making bucket lists if you enjoyed this activity!

Activity 59

A Portrait of a Growth-Minded Me

Congratulations! You've reached the last activity in this workbook. Through the activities in this book, you've learned a lot about the growth mindset and yourself. In celebration of your growth, it is time to complete a portrait of yourself at the end of this journey.

Use the template below to complete a portrait of your face. In the thought bubble above, write as many positive statements about yourself and your growth mindset as you can think of. For example, "I am creative. I can do hard things. I can solve any problem. I make mistakes and learn from them."

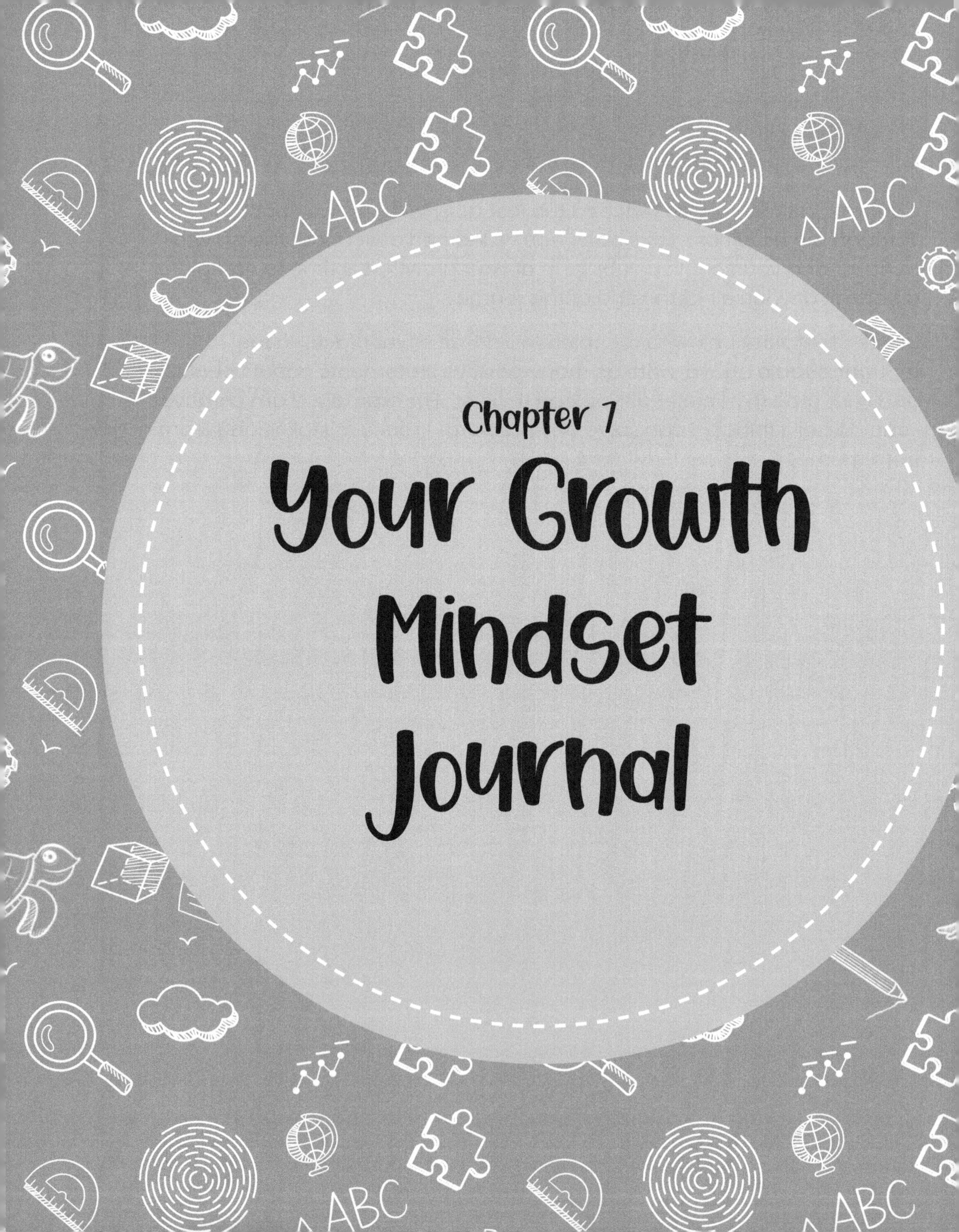

Chapter 7

Your Growth Mindset Journal

In this 7-day journal, we want you to write down all the ways that you're practicing what you learned from this workbook in your daily life. Make note of things that work well and other things that don't work out the way you hoped. Remember – try new ways of doing things and then keep trying! It might be a good idea to review your daily entry with an adult, so they can give you more ideas about how to grow your mind. Have fun journaling about your growth!

Date: ____________

Today is:

Monday	Tuesday	Wednesday	Thursday	Friday	Saturday	Sunday

Some things that happened today are:

Today, I used the following growth mindset behaviors:

- ☐ Having a growth mindset
- ☐ Looking at mistakes as just new challenges
- ☐ The power of yet
- ☐ Incredible problem solving
- ☐ Trying new ways to do things
- ☐ Dreaming big
- ☐ Something I did today that made myself proud: (Or draw it if easier)

One thing I want to do differently next time is:

Date: _______________

Today is:

Monday	Tuesday	Wednesday	Thursday	Friday	Saturday	Sunday

Some things that happened today are:

Today, I used the following growth mindset behaviors:

- ☐ Having a growth mindset
- ☐ Looking at mistakes as just new challenges
- ☐ The power of yet
- ☐ Incredible problem solving
- ☐ Trying new ways to do things
- ☐ Dreaming big
- ☐ Something I did today that made myself proud: (Or draw it if easier)

One thing I want to do differently next time is:

Date: ______________

Today is:

Monday	Tuesday	Wednesday	Thursday	Friday	Saturday	Sunday

Some things that happened today are:

Today, I used the following growth mindset behaviors:

- ☐ Having a growth mindset
- ☐ Looking at mistakes as just new challenges
- ☐ The power of yet
- ☐ Incredible problem solving
- ☐ Trying new ways to do things
- ☐ Dreaming big
- ☐ Something I did today that made myself proud: (Or draw it if easier)

One thing I want to do differently next time is:

DAY 4

Date: ____________

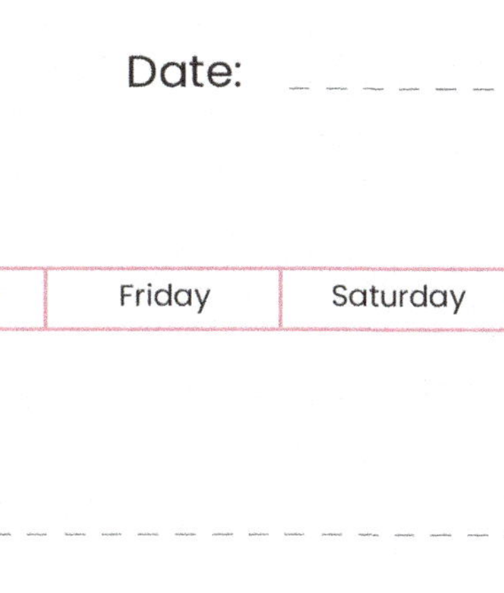

Today is:

Monday	Tuesday	Wednesday	Thursday	Friday	Saturday	Sunday

Some things that happened today are:

____

____

____

____

____

____

____

Today, I used the following growth mindset behaviors:

- ☐ Having a growth mindset
- ☐ Looking at mistakes as just new challenges
- ☐ The power of yet
- ☐ Incredible problem solving
- ☐ Trying new ways to do things
- ☐ Dreaming big
- ☐ Something I did today that made myself proud: (Or draw it if easier)

One thing I want to do differently next time is:

____

____

____

____

Date: _______________

Today is:

Monday	Tuesday	Wednesday	Thursday	Friday	Saturday	Sunday

Some things that happened today are:

Today, I used the following growth mindset behaviors:

- ☐ Having a growth mindset
- ☐ Looking at mistakes as just new challenges
- ☐ The power of yet
- ☐ Incredible problem solving
- ☐ Trying new ways to do things
- ☐ Dreaming big
- ☐ Something I did today that made myself proud: (Or draw it if easier)

One thing I want to do differently next time is:

Date: ______________

Today is:

Monday	Tuesday	Wednesday	Thursday	Friday	Saturday	Sunday

Some things that happened today are:

Today, I used the following growth mindset behaviors:

- ☐ Having a growth mindset
- ☐ Looking at mistakes as just new challenges
- ☐ The power of yet
- ☐ Incredible problem solving
- ☐ Trying new ways to do things
- ☐ Dreaming big
- ☐ Something I did today that made myself proud: (Or draw it if easier)

One thing I want to do differently next time is:

Date: ______________

Today is:

Monday	Tuesday	Wednesday	Thursday	Friday	Saturday	Sunday

Some things that happened today are:

Today, I used the following growth mindset behaviors:

- ☐ Having a growth mindset
- ☐ Looking at mistakes as just new challenges
- ☐ The power of yet
- ☐ Incredible problem solving
- ☐ Trying new ways to do things
- ☐ Dreaming big
- ☐ Something I did today that made myself proud: (Or draw it if easier)

One thing I want to do differently next time is:

TWO SPECIAL GIFTS FOR OUR READERS

AS A SPECIAL THANK YOU FOR STARTING YOUR GROWTH MINDSET JOURNEY, WE'D LIKE TO GIVE YOU:

YOUR OWN GROWTH MINDSET PRINTABLES

8 CAREFULLY CRAFTED ACTIVITIES AND POSTERS THAT YOU CAN COLOR, MARK, AND REALLY MAKE YOUR OWN

+

GROWTH MINDSET JOURNAL PAGES

PRINT OFF AS MANY JOURNAL PAGES AS YOU LIKE TO CONTINUE YOUR GROWTH MINDSET PROGRESS WAY BEYOND THIS BOOK

TO GET YOURS VISIT WWW.DADDILIFE.COM/MYGROWTHMINDSET

Special thanks and useful links

A special thanks to the DaddiLife team for their writing, and to our education experts Ginny Walters and Jocelyn Cunya for their brilliant collaboration across the activities and journal.

A huge thanks too to Emilie for her lovely design work, and to Jon Shortt for his incredible illustrations throughout the book.

Useful Links

As well as this book, there are some amazing online resources for you to get even more Growth Mindset ideas from.

Our favourites include:

Grow Your Mindset Downloadable's: https://www.growyourmindset.co.uk/useful-downloadables

understood.org growth mindset activities: https://www.understood.org/en/articles/download-growth-mindset-activities-for-kids

Rock Your Homeschool activities: https://rockyourhomeschool.net/growth-mindset-activities

Little Owls Growth Mindset resources: https://littleowls-premium.com/growth-mindset

Made in the USA
Las Vegas, NV
12 June 2023

73347186R00083